NATURE'S MYSTERIES

VOLCANOES

SARAH MACHAJEWSKI

Britannica®
Educational Publishing

IN ASSOCIATION WITH

ROSEN
EDUCATIONAL SERVICES

Published in 2017 by Britannica Educational Publishing (a trademark of Encyclopædia Britannica, Inc.) in association with The Rosen Publishing Group, Inc.
29 East 21st Street, New York, NY 10010

Distributed exclusively by Rosen Publishing.
To see additional Britannica Educational Publishing titles, go to rosenpublishing.com.

First Edition

Britannica Educational Publishing
J.E. Luebering: Executive Director, Core Editorial
Mary Rose McCudden: Editor, Britannica Student Encyclopedia

Rosen Publishing
Shalini Saxena: Editor
Nelson Sá: Art Director
Michael Moy: Designer
Cindy Reiman: Photography Manager
Karen Huang: Photo Researcher

Library of Congress Cataloging-in-Publication Data

Names: Machajewski, Sarah, author.
Title: Volcanoes / Sarah Machajewski.
Description: First edition. | New York : Britannica Educational Publishing in
   association with Rosen Educational Services, 2017. | "2017 | Series:
   Nature's mysteries | Audience: Grades 1 to 4. | Includes bibliographical
   references and index.
Identifiers: LCCN 2015044790| ISBN 9781680484847 (library bound : alk. paper)
   | ISBN 9781680484922 (pbk. : alk. paper) | ISBN 9781680484618 (6-pack :
   alk. paper)
Subjects: LCSH: Volcanoes—Juvenile literature. | Volcanism and
   Climate—Juvenile literature. | Volcanology—Juvenile literature.
Classification: LCC QE521.3 .M23 2017 | DDC 551.21—dc23
LC record available at http://lccn.loc.gov/2015044790

Manufactured in the United States of America

Photo Credits: Cover, p. 1 Juan Carlos Muñoz/age fotostock/Getty Images; cover, p. 1 (cloudburst graphic) Macrovector/Shutterstock.com; p. 4 beboy/Shutterstock.com; p. 5 Judie Anderson/EB Inc.; p. 6 Byron Augustin/D. Donne Bryant Stock; p. 7 © Merriam-Webster Inc.; pp. 8, 9, 10, 11, 16 Encyclopædia Britannica, Inc.; p. 12 Kirkendall/Spring; pp. 13, 24 U.S. Geological Survey; p. 14 Hawaii Volcano Observatory/U.S. Geological Survey; p. 15 Adrienne Adam, Fine Art Photographer/Moment Open/Getty Images; p. 17 Ekkachai Pholrojpanya/Moment/Getty Images; pp. 18, 25 Willie Scott/U.S. Geological Survey; p. 19 © AP Images; p. 20 Nigel Hicks/Dorling Kindersley/Getty Images; p. 21 Danita Delimont/Gallo Images/Getty Images; p. 22 Bibliotheque des Arts Decoratifs, Paris, France/Archives Charmet/Bridgeman Images; p. 23 Frans Sellies/Moment/Getty Images; p. 26 Photos.com/Thinkstock; p. 27 © Barbara Whitney; p. 28 Carsten Peter/National Geographic Magazines/Getty Images; p. 29 Heritage Images/Hulton Archive/Getty Images interior pages background patterns Eky Studio/Shutterstock.com (rays), zffoto/Shutterstock.com (waves); back cover, interior pages background image Kamira/Shutterstock.com.

CONTENTS

EARTHLY EXPLOSIONS

Imagine you're looking at a mountain. From the outside, it is big, solid, and steady. Suddenly, great bursts of fire shoot into the air. Clouds of ash and gas roar into the sky. Rivers of lava race down the sides. Now it is clear: that is a volcano, not a mountain!

Volcanoes have fascinated people for centuries. The ancient Romans believed volcanoes erupted

Fiery lava explodes from the mouth of a volcano. Volcanic eruptions are both dangerous and fascinating.

when their god of fire, Vulcan, made thunder-bolts and weapons. Other cultures explained volcanoes as outbursts of anger from a god or goddess. These beliefs were a way to understand something that seemed mysterious.

Today scientists can explain a great deal about volcanic activity. However, it still seems mysterious. Volcanic activity brews underground, beneath our feet, and we cannot see it—until a great explosion forces us to look.

Vulcan was also the god of metalworking. Here, he forges a weapon with fire and tools.

WHAT IS A VOLCANO?

In December 2015, Nicaragua's Momotombo volcano erupted for the first time in 110 years. Until then, it seemed like a quiet mountain.

A volcano is an opening in Earth's crust. When a volcano erupts, hot gases and melted rock from deep within Earth find their way up to the surface. They escape through the opening in the crust.

A volcano often looks like a mountain from the outside. However, on the inside, a volcano is not a solid mass of rock. The opening at the top of the volcano is called a crater. If you were to look down into the crater, you would see a hollow tube called a vent. The vent runs from the crater down into a pool of magma below Earth's surface.

Magma is contained in a space called a magma chamber. When a volcano erupts, the magma travels up through the vent and exits through the crater. Once magma comes aboveground, it is called lava. Some volcanoes may not erupt for hundreds or even thousands of years.

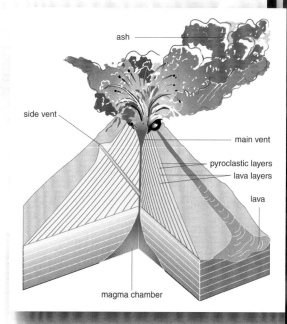

ash

side vent

main vent

pyroclastic layers
lava layers

lava

magma chamber

Volcanoes form when magma beneath Earth's crust forces its way to the surface, as this diagram shows.

A LOOK INSIDE EARTH

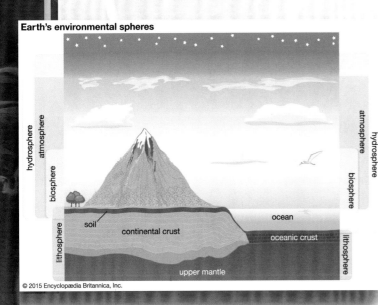

Earth's environmental spheres

atmosphere
hydrosphere
biosphere
lithosphere

atmosphere
hydrosphere
biosphere
lithosphere

soil
continental crust
ocean
oceanic crust
upper mantle

© 2015 Encyclopædia Britannica, Inc.

Earth's volcanoes and other landforms were created over millions of years by the movement of the crust.

To understand volcanoes, it is important to understand the inside of our planet. Earth has many layers. The rocky outer layer is the crust. It sits on top of a layer called the mantle. The mantle has two parts: the upper mantle, or lithosphere, and the lower mantle, or asthenosphere. The lithosphere is cool and hard. The mantle's asthenosphere is hot and soft.

COMPARE AND CONTRAST

The upper mantle and lower mantle have different physical properties. How are they similar? What differences do they have?

Scientists believe Earth is always moving and shifting beneath its surface. According to this theory, Earth's crust and upper mantle are broken into large pieces called tectonic plates. The plates fit together somewhat like pieces of a puzzle. They float on top of the soft, fluid asthenosphere. As the plates move, they rub against each other or move apart along their boundaries. This is where we can begin to understand the mystery of volcanism.

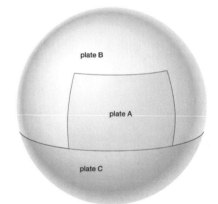

This diagram shows the different ways Earth's plates move and overlap with each other.

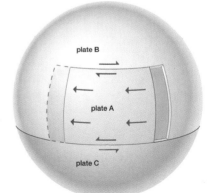

WHERE VOLCANOES FORM

Most volcanoes lie along boundaries between plates. Some of the most violent volcanic eruptions take place where one plate is forced beneath another. This forces magma to rise to the surface. Most volcanoes created like this are found around the Pacific Ocean. This huge chain of volcanoes is known as the Ring of Fire.

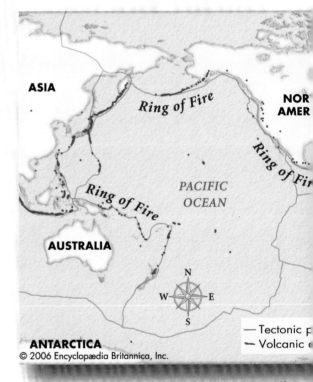

ASIA

Ring of Fire

NOR AMER

Ring of Fire

PACIFIC OCEAN

Ring of Fire

AUSTRALIA

N
W   E
S

ANTARCTICA

© 2006 Encyclopædia Britannica, Inc.

— Tectonic p
— Volcanic

The Ring of Fire circles the Pacific Ocean, hugging the coasts of Asia and North and South America.

An active volcano is a volcano that has had at least one eruption within the last 10,000 years.

There are about 1,500 active volcanoes on Earth, and more than half of them are located here. There are dormant and extinct volcanoes, too.

Volcanoes also form in places where two plates slowly pull apart. Molten rock rises between the plates as they move apart, and lava flows out over the ground. This type of volcano is common along the Mid-Atlantic Ridge, a mountain chain under the Atlantic Ocean. Volcanoes in this ridge formed the island country of Iceland!

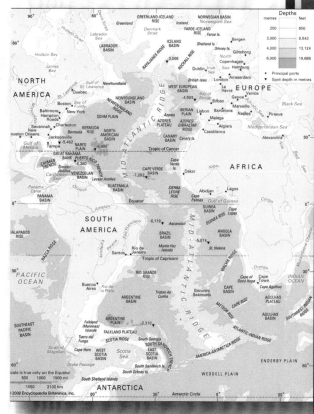

Even though most of it is underwater, the Mid-Atlantic Ridge is part of the longest mountain range in the world.

ALL ABOUT MAGMA

Basalt is a type of rock, formed by cooled lava. Basaltic lava cooled to form the Devils Postpile in California.

Many kinds of geologic activity happen along plate boundaries. Volcanic activity occurs because of magma. Magma forms in the crust and upper mantle. It is created when the temperature in these layers becomes hot enough to melt rock. Magma itself is extremely hot—it can reach temperatures of 2,300 degrees Fahrenheit (1,300 degrees Celsius)!

Magma rises as it forms and collects in a magma chamber. Although magma is a liquid, it also contains gas. Gas bubbles escape from the magma, which creates pressure inside the magma chamber. When the building pressure and heat cause the rock around the magma to start cracking, magma is pushed up through these cracks. It then bursts through to Earth's surface as lava. Fresh lava can be as hot as 2,200 degrees Fahrenheit (1,200 degrees Celsius).

Lava explodes out of Kilauea, the most active volcano in Hawaii. Lava is not actually fire, though its heat might start one.

A LOOK AT LAVA

Volcanoes are fascinating because it looks like they shoot fire into the sky. Some volcanoes seem to pour fire out of their crater. That fire is actually lava, ash, and gas. Lava glows red hot to white as it flows. Some lava flows downhill at 35 miles (56 kilometers) per hour. Other lava moves just inches per day. The speed of the flow depends on what the lava is made of and how hot it is.

Lava cools as it hardens. Hardened lava is called igneous

This lava is moving slowly enough for a scientist to examine it without being hurt.

THINK ABOUT IT

Lava with high gas content creates explosive eruptions, while lava with low gas content flows smoothly. Why does the amount of gas bubbles in the lava affect how it flows?

rock. As new layers of lava cool and harden, they create new landforms. Many islands have been formed by underwater lava flows. The layers of lava grow until the volcano rises above sea level. The Hawaiian Islands and the island of Surtsey, near Iceland, were formed this way.

Hardened lava created the rock formation known as the Giant's Causeway in Northern Ireland.

TYPES OF VOLCANOES

A volcano's shape and size depends on how it erupts. You can tell a lot about a volcano just by looking at it!

Stratovolcanoes are the most common type of volcano. They're steep and made of layers of lava and rock. Stratovolcanoes are known for having violent eruptions.

As volcanoes erupt they create different landforms. Each type has a different name.

Volcanic Landforms

shield volcano

stratovolcano

complex volcano

caldera

somma volcano

COMPARE AND CONTRAST

Consider how cinder cone volcanoes, stratovolcanoes, and shield volcanoes look and erupt. How are they the same? How are they different?

Shield volcanoes are dome-shaped formations built of lava flows. They are created by thin lava that flows from a vent and spreads over a wide area. Cinder cone volcanoes are steep and are built of loose rock fragments.

Volcanic explosions can create new landforms, including calderas. A caldera is formed when a volcano erupts most of what is in its magma chamber. Without anything to support it, the crater collapses inward and creates a large sunken area.

The caldera in front of Mount Semeru in Indonesia was created by an ancient volcano.

IN THE WAKE OF AN ERUPTION

Volcanic ash from Mount Pinatubo covers Clark Air Base in the Philippines.

An erupting volcano is spectacular to watch but only at a safe distance. Eruptions are extremely dangerous and even deadly.

Strong volcanic eruptions throw bits of magma into the air. Wind can carry volcanic dust thousands of miles away. Volcanic ash can coat the land for miles around the volcano.

Steam and poisonous gases also escape from

THINK ABOUT IT
Flowing rivers of lava and huge clouds of ash and gas can spread out miles from a volcano. What could happen to a city or town that is close to an eruption?

volcanoes. Sometimes these gases are mixed with ash and other hot particles. This mixture travels outward in destructive fiery clouds, called pyroclastic flows.

Enormous amounts of lava, enough to flood the area surrounding the volcano, can be produced during a major volcanic eruption. In some cases, people living around an active volcano must leave the area in order to stay safe. They may lose their homes, but they do not want to lose their lives.

Families living near the Cotopaxi volcano in Ecuador get ready to leave their homes as ash fills the sky.

LONG-LASTING EFFECTS

Very strong eruptions can change the planet's climate. Particles of gas and ash can become trapped in Earth's atmosphere. Sometimes this blocks out the Sun, making Earth cooler. This change can be temporary, or it can last for hundreds of years! That's what scientists think caused Earth's Little Ice Age, which lasted from about 1300 to the late 1800s.

Scientists think that beginning in about 1300, several

Scientists believe that the 1783 eruptions of Mount Laki in Iceland may have contributed to the Little Ice Age.

major volcanic eruptions happened over a 50-year period. The unusual amount of eruptions in a short time put so many particles into the air that they cooled the planet for centuries.

Volcanoes are not entirely harmful, though. Soil that has volcanic ash is very rich and good for growing crops. Obsidian, or volcanic glass, has been used to make weapons, tools, and ornaments. Pumice, or volcanic rock, is used as a cleaning tool and for building materials.

Fertile volcanic soil allows rice crops to grow healthy and strong on the island of Bali in Indonesia.

FAMOUS ERUPTIONS

S ome volcanic eruptions stand out more than others. They are usually the most destructive and have the greatest impact on people's lives.

In 79 CE Mount Vesuvius, in southern Italy, erupted so suddenly and so violently that it buried entire cities! Thousands of people died when lava, ashes, and mud buried the Roman cities of Pompeii, Herculaneum, and Stabiae. After two days, Pompeii was

The ancient city of Pompeii was destroyed when Mount Vesuvius erupted in 79 CE.

Archaeologists are scientists who want to understand what the people of the past were like and how they lived.

buried under 19 to 23 feet (6 to 7 meters) of ash and volcanic stone.

Archaeologists began uncovering the city's ruins in the 1700s. They found the city preserved as it was on the day of the blast. Casts of bodies, animals, tools, and even loaves of bread were found intact. These finds have taught us a lot about life in ancient Pompeii.

Visitors can now see the ruins of Pompeii and the nearby cities. These ruins have taught us much about ancient Roman life.

Mount Saint Helens, a volcano in the state of Washington, erupted on May 18, 1980. It was one of the greatest volcanic explosions ever recorded in North America.

On the day of the eruption, an earthquake caused a landslide on the mountain. This was followed by a blast of hot ash and stone that was thrown about 15 miles (24 kilometers) from the volcano. The blast reached speeds of 300 miles (483 kilometers) per hour.

The mountain and surrounding landscape were completely changed after the eruption. Landslides and lava flow flattened forests and carried debris as far

Smoke and ash pour out of Mount Saint Helens in this 1980 photograph.

as 17 miles (27 kilometers) away. Sadly, 57 people and thousands of animals were killed.

Another volcano in Iceland erupted in 2010 and caused major problems for travelers throughout the world. The volcano produced a huge ash cloud that spread to the east. It caused many airports in Europe to close because it was too dangerous for planes to fly through the ash.

Today, Mount Saint Helens has a huge crater from the explosion that happened in 1980.

OTHER TYPES OF VOLCANIC ACTIVITY

A hot spring is a place where warm water comes up through the ground. Hot springs are found in areas with volcanic activity. The heat from magma warms underground water. Some hot springs are safe for swimming!

A geyser is a kind of hot spring that sends steam and hot water gushing into the air. Geysers erupt when magma heats water underground. When the water boils, it turns into steam. The steam expands, creates pressure, and pushes water up

The water of Old Faithful can be as hot as 205 degrees Fahrenheit (96 degrees Celsius).

and out of Earth with great force. Old Faithful in Yellowstone National Park is a famous geyser that erupts regularly.

A fumarole is an opening in the ground that releases steam and gases. Fumaroles are also found on active volcanoes between eruptions. The steam comes from groundwater that is heated by magma. Nearly all the water is turned to steam, so no water escapes. Hot springs, geysers, and fumaroles are caused by the same activity that makes volcanoes explode!

Steam rolls out of this fumarole, which is located in Iceland.

MYSTERY NOT SOLVED

Volcanism might seem like one of nature's greatest mysteries. One of the best ways to solve a mystery is to investigate it. That's exactly what **volcanologists** do.

Many volcanologists work in observatories where they keep track of signs of volcanic activity. This includes tracking movement inside Earth. Some volcanologists actually visit volcanoes and craters for an even closer

A volcanologist takes samples from Mount Nyriagongo in the Democratic Republic of the Congo.

look. Based on what they see, they try to predict when an eruption might take place, how violent it would be, and which areas would be in danger.

Volcanologists have helped uncover some of the mystery behind volcanism. We have even learned how to heat homes using hot water from volcanic springs. But there is much to learn about when eruptions occur and how they affect the Earth and climate. Like people long ago, we may still not know exactly when an eruption will happen, but we remain fascinated by volcanoes.

Visitors take a guided tour of Mount Etna, a volcano in Italy. A tour is a great way to see a volcano up close!

GLOSSARY

ATMOSPHERE The layer of gases surrounding Earth and other bodies in space.

BOUNDARIES Lines that mark where an area begins and ends.

CLIMATE The average weather conditions in an area over a long period of time.

DESTRUCTIVE Causing great harm or damage.

DORMANT VOLCANOES Volcanoes that have not erupted in 10,000 years but are expected to erupt in the future.

EXTINCT VOLCANOES Volcanoes that have not erupted in 10,000 years and are not likely to erupt again.

GEOLOGIC Having to do with Earth's physical properties and the processes that act on it.

ICE AGE A time when thick ice sheets cover huge areas of land.

INVESTIGATE To study something in order to learn more about it.

LANDSLIDE An event when a mass of earth or rocks slides down the side of a mountain or cliff.

LAYER A covering piece of material or a part that lies over or under another.

PREDICT To say how something will be in the future.

PRESERVED Kept in its original state.

PRESSURE The weight or force that is produced when something presses or pushes against something else.

SPECTACULAR Beautiful or eye-catching.

TEMPERATURE The measure of how hot or cold something is.

FOR MORE INFORMATION

Books

Coleman, Miriam. *Investigating Volcanoes*. New York, NY: PowerKids Press, 2015.

Ganeri, Anita. *Violent Volcanoes*. New York, NY: Scholastic, 2015.

Hyde, Natalie. *Earthquakes, Eruptions, and Other Events that Change Earth*. St. Catherines, ON, Canada: Crabtree Publishing, 2015.

Katigiris, Jane. *Volatile Volcanoes*. Berkeley Heights, NJ: Enslow Publishers, 2015.

Smith, Kelly. *How Hot Is Lava? And Other Questions About Volcanoes*. New York, NY: Sterling Children's Books, 2016.

Websites

Because of the changing nature of Internet links, Rosen Publishing has developed an online list of websites related to the subject of this book. This site is updated regularly. Please use this link to access this list:

http://www.rosenlinks.com/NMY/volcan

INDEX